I0413283

NISTIR 7585

Evaluation of Oral Fluid Testing Devices

Lorna T. Sniegoski
Jocelyn Waddell
Michael J. Welch
Alim A. Fatah*
National Institute of Standards and Technology
Chemical Science and Technology Laboratory

Coordination by:
U.S. DEPARTMENT OF COMMERCE
*Office of Law Enforcement Standards
National Institute of Standards
    and Technology
Gaithersburg, MD 20899–8102

Mae Gackstetter
Robert Q. Thompson
Department of Chemistry
Oberlin College
Oberlin, OH 44074

National Institute of
Standards and Technology
U.S. Department of Commerce

ABOUT THE LAW ENFORCEMENT AND CORRECTIONS STANDARDS AND TESTING PROGRAM

The Law Enforcement and Corrections Standards and Testing Program is sponsored by the Office of Science and Technology of the National Institute of Justice (NIJ), U.S. Department of Justice. The program responds to the mandate of the Justice System Improvement Act of 1979, which created NIJ and directed it to encourage research and development to improve the criminal justice system and to disseminate the results to Federal, State, and local agencies.

The Law Enforcement and Corrections Standards and Testing Program is an applied research effort that determines the technological needs of justice system agencies, sets minimum performance standards for specific devices, tests commercially available equipment against those standards, and disseminates the standards and the test results to criminal justice agencies nationally and internationally.

The program operates through:

The *Law Enforcement and Corrections Technology Advisory Council* (LECTAC) consisting of nationally recognized criminal justice practitioners from Federal, State, and local agencies, which assesses technological needs and sets priorities for research programs and items to be evaluated and tested.

The *Office of Law Enforcement Standards* (OLES) at the National Institute of Standards and Technology, which develops voluntary national performance standards for compliance testing to ensure that individual items of equipment are suitable for use by criminal justice agencies. The standards are based upon laboratory testing and evaluation of representative samples of each item of equipment to determine the key attributes, develop test methods, and establish minimum performance requirements for each essential attribute. In addition to the highly technical standards, OLES also produces technical reports and user guidelines that explain in nontechnical terms the capabilities of available equipment.

The *National Law Enforcement and Corrections Technology Center* (NLECTC), operated by a grantee, which supervises a national compliance testing program conducted by independent laboratories. The standards developed by OLES serve as performance benchmarks against which commercial equipment is measured. The facilities, personnel, and testing capabilities of the independent laboratories are evaluated by OLES prior to testing each item of equipment, and OLES helps the NLECTC staff review and analyze data. Test results are published in Equipment Performance Reports designed to help justice system procurement officials make informed purchasing decisions.

Publications are available at no charge through the National Law Enforcement and Corrections Technology Center. Some documents are also available online through the Internet/World Wide Web. To request a document or additional information, call 800–248–2742 or 301–519–5060, or write:

National Law Enforcement and Corrections Technology Center
P.O. Box 1160
Rockville, MD 20849–1160
E-Mail: *asknlectc@nlectc.org*
World Wide Web address: *http://www.nlectc.org*

This document is not intended to create, does not create, and may not be relied upon to create any rights, substantive or procedural, enforceable at law by any party in any matter civil or criminal.

Opinions or points of view expressed in this document represent a consensus of the authors and do not represent the official position or policies of the U.S. Department of Justice. The products and manufacturers discussed in this document are presented for informational purposes only and do not constitute product approval or endorsement by the U.S. Department of Justice.

NISTIR 7585

Evaluation of Oral Fluid Testing Devices

Lorna T. Sniegoski
Jocelyn Waddell
Michael J. Welch
Alim A. Fatah
National Institute of Standards and Technology
Chemical Science and Technology Laboratory

Coordination by:
U.S. DEPARTMENT OF COMMERCE
Office of Law Enforcement Standards
National Institute of Standards
  and Technology
Gaithersburg, MD 20899–8102

Mae Gackstetter
Robert Q. Thompson
Department of Chemistry
Oberlin College
Oberlin, OH 44074

April 2009

U.S. DEPARTMENT OF COMMERCE
Carlos M. Gutierrez, Secretary

NATIONAL INSTITUTE OF STANDARDS
AND TECHNOLOGY
Patrick D. Gallagher, Deputy Director

ACKNOWLEDGMENTS

The technical effort to develop this report was conducted under Interagency Agreement 2003–IJ–R–029, Project No. 08–004.

This research was funded by the National Institute of Justice through the Office of Law Enforcement Standards (OLES) of the National Institute of Standards and Technology (NIST).

This report was conducted under the direction of Alim A. Fatah, Program Manager for Chemical Systems and Materials, and Mark D. Stolorow, Director of OLES.

FOREWORD

The Office of Law Enforcement Standards (OLES) of the National Institute of Standards and Technology (NIST) furnishes technical support to the National Institute of Justice (NIJ) program to strengthen law enforcement and criminal justice in the United States. OLES's function is to develop standards and conduct research that will assist law enforcement and criminal justice agencies in the selection and procurement of quality equipment.

OLES is: (1) Subjecting existing equipment to laboratory testing and evaluation, and (2) conducting research leading to the development of several series of documents, including national standards, user guides, and technical reports.

This document covers research conducted by OLES under the sponsorship of the NIJ. Additional reports as well as other documents are being issued under the OLES program in the areas of protective clothing and equipment, communications systems, emergency equipment, investigative aids, security systems, vehicles, weapons, and analytical techniques and standard reference materials used by the forensic community.

Technical comments and suggestions concerning this report are invited from all interested parties. They may be addressed to the Office of Law Enforcement Standards, National Institute of Standards and Technology, 100 Bureau Drive, Stop 8102, Gaithersburg, MD 20899–8102.

Mark D. Stolorow, Director
Office of Law Enforcement Standards

CONTENTS

TABLES

FIGURES

COMMONLY USED SYMBOLS AND ABBREVIATIONS

A	Ampere	hf	high frequency	Ω	ohm
ac	alternating current	Hz	hertz	p.	page
AM	amplitude modulation	i.d.	inside diameter	Pa	pascal
Amu	atomic mass unit	in	inch	Pe	probable error
cd	Candela	IR	infrared	pp.	pages
cm	Centimeter	J	joule	Ppm	parts per million
CP	chemically pure	L	lambert	Qt	quart
c/s	cycle per second	L	liter	Rad	radian
d	day	lb	pound	Rf	radio frequency
dB	decibel	lbf	pound-force	Rh	relative humidity
dc	direct current	lbf·in	pound-force inch	S	second
°C	degree Celsius	lm	lumen	SD	standard deviation
°F	degree Fahrenheit	ln	logarithm (base e)	sec.	Section
dia	diameter	log	logarithm (base 10)	SWR	standing wave ratio
emf	electromotive force	M	molar	uhf	ultrahigh frequency
eq	equation	m	meter	UV	ultraviolet
F	farad	μ	micron	V	volt
fc	footcandle	min	minute	vhf	very high frequency
fig.	Figure	mm	millimeter	W	watt
FM	frequency modulation	mph	miles per hour	λ	wavelength
ft	foot	m/s	meter per second	wk	week
ft/s	foot per second	mo	month	wt	weight
g	acceleration	N	newton	yr	year
g	gram	N·m	newton meter		
gr	grain	nm	nanometer		
H	henry	No.	Number		
h	hour	o.d.	outside diameter		

area=unit^2 (e.g., ft^2, in^2, etc.); volume=unit^3 (e.g., ft^3, m^3, etc.)

PREFIXES (See ASTM E380)

d	deci (10^{-1})	da	deka (10)
c	centi (10^{-2})	h	hecto (10^2)
m	milli (10^{-3})	k	kilo (10^3)
μ	micro (10^{-6})	M	mega (10^6)
n	nano (10^{-9})	G	giga (10^9)
p	pico (10^{-12})	T	tera (10^{12})

COMMON CONVERSIONS

0.30480 m = 1 ft	4.448222 N = 1 lbf
25.4 mm = 1 in	1.355818 J = 1 ft·lbf
0.4535924 kg = 1 lb	0.1129848 N m = 1 lbf·in
0.06479891g = 1gr	14.59390 N/m = 1 lbf/ft
0.9463529 L = 1 qt	6894.757 Pa = 1 lbf/in^2
3600000 J = 1 kW·hr	1.609344 km/h = 1 mph
psi = mm of Hg x (1.9339×10^{-2})	
mm of Hg = psi x 51.71	

Temperature: $T_C = (T_F - 32) \times 5/9$ Temperature: $T_F = (T_C \times 9/5) + 32$

DISCLAIMER

Certain commercial equipment, instruments, or materials are identified in this paper in order to specify the experimental procedure adequately. Such identification is not intended to imply recommendation or endorsement by the National Institute of Standards and Technology (NIST), nor is it intended to imply that the materials or equipment identified are necessarily the best available for the purpose.

1. INTRODUCTION

Oral fluid (saliva) testing is becoming increasingly popular as a means for quickly determining if someone might be under the influence of drugs or alcohol. Collection of saliva specimens is noninvasive, compared to blood and nonintrusive with regards to the privacy of the subject when compared to urine collection. In addition, no special facilities or training are required in order to obtain the saliva specimen and supervised sample collection eliminates the possibility of sample adulteration. Drug detection is possible within a few hours to a full day from initial use, a timeframe similar to blood samples. The market for these tests is dominated by small, single use devices. For drugs of abuse testing, the instructions include a disclaimer that a positive use test must be confirmed by more rigorous laboratory tests.

NIST undertook a study of oral fluid testing devices for detecting alcohol (ethanol) and for detecting common drugs of abuse. This report provides details of the two studies. Five devices intended for detecting alcohol in oral fluid were evaluated in terms of their accuracy in detecting varying levels of ethanol in oral fluid. The ability of the devices to reliably detect ethanol in the presence of potential interfering substances was also assessed.

Four point-of-collection (POC) devices for detection of drugs of abuse in oral fluid were also studied. The ability of the devices to meet the manufacturers' claims and their practical application to detection of drugs of abuse at low concentrations in oral fluid were evaluated. Human saliva fortified with known quantities of cocaine, phencyclidine (PCP), codeine, morphine, amphetamine, methamphetamine, and ($\pm$)-11-nor-9-carboxy-Δ^9-tetrahydrocannabinol (carboxy-THC), was used in the analysis. Each device was also tested for cross-reactivity with a number of common orally administered, over the counter medications, as well as substances which could be expected to occur in human saliva. In general, the POC devices performed close to their specifications, with a few exceptions. In some cases, the design of the device could make interpretation of the results unreliable or uncertain.

2. DEVICES FOR TESTING FOR ALCOHOL

2.1 Experimental Procedures for Ethanol-Water Solutions

2.1.1 Preparation of Standard Solutions in Water

Since the legal limit for of-age Driving Under Influence (DUI) in most of the states in the United States is 0.080 g ethanol per 100 mL blood (0.080 %), four or five standards with nominal concentrations bracketing that value (0.02 % to 0.50 %, mass/volume fraction) were chosen for calibration. Nominal concentrations were reported in % (g ethanol per 100 mL water) while exact concentration in units of mg ethanol per g solution were plotted and used in data analysis.

Each ethanol and propanol standard solution was prepared in the following manner. An appropriate amount of ethanol (99.5 % (mass fraction) purity, Sigma, St. Louis, MO) was added to a 250-mL volumetric flask, and the flask was filled with 18 MΩ purified water from a water purifier (Barnstead, Dubuque, IA). The masses of ethanol and water were measured on balances calibrated with mass standards traceable to NIST. After thorough mixing, 40 mL of the standard was transferred to a septum-capped vial and stored at 4 °C. 1-propanol was chosen as the internal standard, and a 0.10 g per 100 mL water solution was prepared in a similar manner.

Test solutions were prepared by transferring with a syringe (through the septum cap) 0.5 mL of ethanol standard solution (allowed to warm to room temperature) or sample or blank (water) and 0.5 mL of 1-propanol standard solution (allowed to warm to room temperature) to a septum-capped vial. The masses of each of the standard solutions were measured on a calibrated analytical balance.

2.1.2 Gas Chromatographic Method for Ethanol-Water Solutions

A gas chromatographic method was developed for determination of ethanol levels in oral fluids. A Hewlett-Packard (HP) 5890 Series II gas chromatograph equipped with an FID detector and attached to an HP model 3395 recording integrator was used. Manual injections of 1 μL were split 22:1 in the split injection port (4-mm, with cup and glass wool, split injection liner). Injector and detector temperatures were 200 °C. The column was a 15 m x 0.25 mm AT-WAX fused silica capillary column with a stationary phase thickness of 0.50 μm. The oven program was 35 °C for 2.0 min, ramp 1 of 15 °C/min to 80 °C, ramp 2 of 40 °C/min to 120 °C, hold at 120 °C for 2.0 min. The total run time was 8.0 min. The helium carrier gas had a flow rate of 1.6 mL/min through the column at a head pressure of 60 kPa and a total flow rate of 50 mL/min.

2.1.3 Calculation of Peak Area Ratio, the Measure Directly Related to Analyte Concentration

An internal standard approach was used for quantitation. To correct for variations in injection volume, calculations were based on relative response factors that employed 1-propanol as the internal standard. In practice, the peak area ratio for the analyte (ethanol) to the internal standard (1-propanol) is proportional to the mass ratio for the analyte to the internal standard.

2.1.4 Linear Range

Ethanol standards of nominal concentrations 0.05 % to 7.5 % (mass fractions, corresponding to 0 % to 2.0 % ethanol in the standard solutions) were tested by GC-FID. All of the calibration standard solutions were within the linear range of the method.

2.1.5 Detection Limit

To determine the detection limit of ethanol, two dilute solutions were prepared so as to give signal to noise (S/N) ratios between 4-10 and 50-100. Six injections of each dilute solution were made, and the average peak area ratio served as the signal, and the standard deviation served as the value for noise. This data was fit to a line, and the ethanol concentration corresponding to S/N = 3 was calculated as the detection limit. The 0.02 % (mass fraction) ethanol standard gave the higher S/N ratio of 57 and a 5.4-fold dilution of this standard produced the lower value with a S/N of 7. The detection limit of ethanol was determined to be 0.001 % (mass fraction).

2.1.6 Repeatability Study

Four ethanol standard solutions of nominal concentrations 0.020 %, 0.080 %, 0.20 %, and 0.50 % (mass fractions) plus a blank (water) were prepared. Each standard plus blank was tested three times (three injections) on three consecutive days, and the peak area ratios were recorded. For all ethanol levels, the within-day variation of the peak area ratios was no different from the between-day variation as determined by ANOVA. The precision (relative standard deviation) for the combined (within- and between-day) data was on average 0.9 % for the three higher ethanol concentrations. The relative standard deviation increased quite a bit, to 12 %, for the lowest concentration (0.020 %).

The sensitivity, specificity, efficiency, positive predicative value and negative value were determined for each set of data. Each parameter is defined as follows:

$$ST = \frac{TP}{(TP + FN)} \qquad \text{Eq 1}$$

$$SP = \frac{TN}{(TN + FP)} \qquad \text{Eq 2}$$

$$EF = \frac{TP + TN}{(Total\,Tests)} \qquad \text{Eq 3}$$

$$PPV = \frac{TP}{(TP + FP)} \qquad \text{Eq 4}$$

$$NPV = \frac{TN}{(TN + FP)} \qquad \text{Eq 5}$$

ST = Sensitivity
TP = True Positive
FN = False Negative
TN = True Negatives
FP = False Positives
SP = Specificity
EF = Efficiency
PPV = Positive Predicative Value
NPV = Negative Predicative Value

2.1.7 Recovery Study

Experiments were performed to determine the accuracy of the method in measuring ethanol added to a known ethanol standard prepared in water. A 0.10 % (mass fraction) ethanol solution was prepared in a 100-mL volumetric flask. A 0.50-mL aliquot was taken and combined with 1-propanol internal standard solution for GC-FID analysis. To the remaining ethanol solution was added 50 mg of pure ethanol to increase the concentration to about 0.15 % (mass fraction). A 0.50-mL aliquot of this spiked ethanol solution was taken and combined with 1-propanol internal standard solution for GC-FID analysis. The test solutions were injected twice each on two consecutive days. The resultant blank-corrected area ratios were averaged and used to calculate the ethanol concentrations by comparison to the calibration line generated on the final day of the repeatability study. The calibration line was computed by unweighted linear regression.

The amount of ethanol in the original solution was subtracted from the measured amount of ethanol in the spiked solution to give the amount of ethanol added. The measured amount was divided by the gravimetric amount of ethanol added to determine the fractional recovery. The fractional recovery was 1.016 ± 0.055 (mean ± 1 SD).

2.1.8 Quantitative Study

The accuracy of the GC-FID method was assessed by determining the concentration of ethanol in two levels of Standard Reference Material (SRM) 1828b Ethanol-Water Solutions (Blood-Alcohol Testing: Six Levels). One ampoule of each level of SRM was opened, and the liquid was immediately transferred to a septum-capped vial. The liquid was removed with a syringe for testing. Four ethanol calibration solutions of nominal concentrations 0.020 %, 0.080 %, 0.20 %, and 0.50 % (mass fractions) plus a blank (water) were prepared. Each sample, calibrant, and blank was tested twice on each of two consecutive days.

Calibration measurements provided an excellent fit using an unweighted linear regression model. The measured concentration of ethanol in the Level 1 sample (mean ± 1 SD) was 0.0188 ± 0.0020 g ethanol per 100 g solution as compared to the certified value of 0.0195 ± 0.0002. The certified value was within the 95 % confidence interval (df = 6) of the measured value. The measured concentration of ethanol in the Level 3 sample (mean ± 1 SD) was 0.2904 ± 0.0019 g ethanol per 100 g solution as compared to a certified value of 0.298 ± 0.003 (95 % confidence interval). The certified value was outside the 95 % confidence interval for the measured value. The percent error for Level 3 was -2.5 %. The sensitivity, specificity, efficiency, positive predicative value and negative value were determined for each set of data.

2.2 Experimental Procedures for Oral Fluid

2.2.1 Collection and Preparation of Oral Fluid

Since oral fluid was the medium used with the various drug detection devices under evaluation, the GC-FID method previously developed for use with ethanol water mixtures was verified for oral fluid. Oral fluid was obtained by expectoration from healthy volunteers. Nothing was introduced into the mouths of volunteers for at least 1 h prior to oral fluid collection. The collected oral fluid was pooled and frozen within 1 h of collection. The combined pool was generated over a 5-d period. The oral fluid was thawed and refrozen twice to reduce foaming and then was centrifuged for 30 min in a clinical centrifuge to remove suspended solids. The supernatant was separated and centrifuged for another 20 min. The resulting final supernatant was stored in a sealed container at 4 °C and served as the source of oral fluid in all subsequent studies.

2.2.2 Preparation of Standard Solutions, Spiked Oral Fluid, and Test Solutions

Ethanol standards used to spike the oral fluid were prepared in distilled water as described in Section 2.1.1 at concentrations ranging from 0.1 % to 10 % (mass fractions).

Spiked oral fluid solutions were prepared by pipetting 0.5 mL of oral fluid to a vial with a septum lined cap, and adding 50 µL of the ethanol standard in water (transferred through the septum with a syringe). The masses of each liquid were measured on a calibrated analytical balance.

Test solutions were prepared by adding 0.5 mL of 1-propanol internal standard solution to the spiked oral fluid. The internal standard solution was transferred to the vial through the septum with a syringe, and its mass determined.

2.2.3 Gas Chromatographic Method for Oral Fluid

The method detailed in 2.1.2 was modified for the analysis of oral fluids. The GC program was amended to include an additional temperature ramp to ensure that no substances from the oral fluid were retained on the column. The third ramp was set at 25 °C/min until 220 °C and held for 4.00 min, for a total run time of 16.00 min.

No significant differences were observed in chromatograms of oral fluids or water based samples, in the time range of interest. The retention times for ethanol and 1-propanol were unaffected, and the baseline remained stable. Small peaks from undetermined compounds were detected at 8.1 min and 12.9 min.

2.2.4 Linear Range

Ethanol standards in oral fluid were tested using the GC-FID method described. Spiked oral fluid with nominal ethanol concentrations 0.04 % to 10 % (mass fraction) was tested. The linear range for ethanol in spiked oral fluid was 0 % to 2.0 % (mass fraction).

2.2.5 Detection Limit

The detection limit was determined by preparing a dilute solution of ethanol in oral fluid that gave a S/N ≈ 3. Six injections of the spiked oral fluid solution were made with the average peak area ratio serving as the signal and the standard deviation serving as the value for noise. An ethanol concentration of 0.002 % (mass fraction) in spiked oral fluid gave a S/N ratio of 2.9, close to a S/N ratio of 3 that was designated as the detection limit.

2.2.6 Repeatability Study

Four ethanol standards of nominal concentrations 0.04 %, 0.16 %, 0.40 % and 1.0 % (mass fractions) in spiked oral fluid plus a blank containing only oral fluid were prepared. Each sample was injected three times on three consecutive days and peak area ratios were recorded. The blank showed no peak at the ethanol retention time. For all ethanol levels, the within-day variation of the peak area ratios was no different from the between-day variation as determined by ANOVA. The precision (relative standard deviation) for the combined (within- and between-day) data was on average was less than 2.5 % for all ethanol concentrations, with the largest uncertainty at each end of the concentration range.

2.2.7 Quantitative Study

Five ethanol standards of spiked oral fluid concentrations (nominal) 0.01 %, 0.02 %, 0.08 %, 0.20 % and 0.50 % (mass fractions) were prepared. Each standard plus a blank (oral fluid) was tested twice on two consecutive days. Standard solutions were identical on the two days, but fresh spiked oral fluid and test solutions were prepared each day. Data analysis of these solutions gave a linear plot with a correlation coefficient of 0.9995 each day (see table 2).

2.2.8 Robustness

Test solutions were prepared with slightly different amounts of oral fluid (0.4 mL - 0.6 mL) to determine if the amount of oral fluid influenced the results. No significant differences in the detector response (peak area ratio) per amount of ethanol injected were found. Both low (0.02 % mass fraction) and high (0.20 % mass fraction) nominal ethanol concentrations in spiked oral fluid were tested.

A test solution was left at room temperature for 3 d and then reanalyzed to check whether possible enzyme action and/or bacterial growth over that time frame affected the results. The 0.02 % (mass fraction) ethanol test solution showed no significant difference in the GC-FID peak area ratios over the 3 day period.

2.2.9 Recovery Study

Experiments were performed to determine the accuracy of the method in measuring ethanol added to oral fluid. A 0.5-mL aliquot of spiked oral fluid (0.02 % mass fraction ethanol) was mixed with 0.5 mL 1-propanol internal standard solution and analyzed by GC-FID with duplicate injections. A known amount of 0.8 % (mass fraction) aqueous ethanol standard was added to the remaining test solution, thereby increasing the ethanol concentration in the spiked oral fluid to about 0.10 % (mass fraction). The spiked test solution was injected in duplicate. The peak area ratios were averaged and used to calculate measured ethanol concentrations by unweighted linear regression.

The amount of ethanol in the original solution was subtracted from the measured amount of ethanol in the spiked solution to obtain the amount of ethanol added. The measured amount of ethanol was divided by the gravimetric amount of ethanol added to determine the fractional recovery. The recovery was 0.931 ± 0.040 (mean ± 1 SD).

The recovery study was repeated in the same manner as above but with a smaller addition of ethanol, this time using a 0.2 % (mass fraction) ethanol standard. Thus, the ethanol concentration changed from 0.02 % to 0.04 % (mass fraction). The measured recovery was 1.03 ± 0.19 (mean ± 1 SD). The uncertainty was increased due to the larger relative uncertainty associated with smaller quantities of added ethanol.

2.3 Evaluation of Device Sensitivity for the Determination of Ethanol in Oral Fluid

2.3.1 Preparation of Solutions for Device Testing

Five standard solutions of spiked oral fluid, with nominal ethanol concentrations of 0.01 %, 0.02 %, 0.03 %, 0.08 % and 0.12 % (g ethanol / 100 g spiked oral fluid) were prepared by mixing 15 mL of oral fluid (exact mass known) with 1.5 mL of the appropriate aqueous ethanol standard (exact mass known).

Ethanol standards used to spike the oral fluid were prepared in high purity water as described in section 2.1.1 at nominal concentrations: 0.1 %, 0.2 %, 0.3 %, 0.8 % and 1.2 % (g ethanol / 100 g aqueous standard).

For each of the testing devices, a 0.5-mL aliquot of spiked oral fluid was pipetted to a 10-mL beaker. To prepare a test solution for GC-FID, a 0.5-mL aliquot of spiked oral fluid was transferred with a syringe to a septum-capped vial and weighed. Then, a 0.5 mL aliquot of 1-propanol internal standard solution (0.10 g/100 mL in water) was added with a syringe to the same vial and weighed. Fresh aliquots of spiked oral fluid and test solutions were prepared each time a device was tested.

The test devices refer to percent ethanol concentrations that generally are interpreted as the equivalent blood alcohol level in units of g ethanol / 100 mL of blood. The units used in this report are g ethanol / 100 g fluid and no correction factor for equivalent blood alcohol levels has been applied. The ratio of oral fluid ethanol concentration to blood ethanol concentration for samples obtained simultaneously has been found to be approximately 1.08 (Gubala, *et al. Pol. J. Pharmacol.* 2002, *54*, 161-165), so the oral fluid concentration is a very good indicator of blood alcohol concentration (BAC).

2.3.2 Procedure for Testing the Devices

Each of the five devices was tested with spiked oral fluid at each of the five ethanol concentrations (described above) plus a blank (oral fluid without added aqueous ethanol). Five trials at each of the concentrations were performed for each device, and a test solution that was injected into the GC-FID accompanied each test. The QED A150 testing swab was placed in the oral fluid for 45 s as specified by the manufacturer. All the other devices were placed in the oral fluid for 15 s to saturate the test pad; saturation with oral fluid was specified by the manufacturers. For specific details and testing procedures of each device, see below.

Device	Manufacturer	Response Category
QED A150	Orasure Technologies	Quantitative
Alco-Screen	Chematics	Semi-Quantitative
Alco-Screen 02	Chematics	Qualitative
Rapid Response	Biotechnostix	Qualitative
OnSite	Varian	Qualitative

QED A150

The QED A150 Saliva Alcohol Test manufactured by Orasure Technologies, Inc., is designed to provide a quantitative determination of blood alcohol concentration (BAC) in 2 min from a fresh oral fluid sample. The QED A150 is capable of determining alcohol levels in the range of 0.01 % to 0.145 % (g ethanol / 100 mL of blood, [units assumed]) with a reading precision of 0.005 %. The device works by an enzymatic method. Alcohol dehydrogenase catalyzes the oxidation of alcohol to acetaldehyde and reduces NAD to NADH at the same time. An alkaline pH and acetaldehyde trapping agent are employed to ensure that the reaction generates one mole of NADH for each mole of ethanol in the sample. Diaphorase, an unspecified oxidizing agent, and a tetrazolium salt are all incorporated into a solid reagent, which reacts with the NADH to form a colored product (formazan dye).

The QED A150 test package was opened immediately prior to use. The instructions for use state that devices are to be discarded if the QA Spot (a quality control indicator at the top of the device's scale) is purple or the desiccant package is pink; however, none of the packages had to be discarded. The instructions for use specify that the swab should be actively rubbed around the mouth and under the tongue for 30 s to 60 s or until the swab was saturated. To replicate these conditions, a swab was placed in the 0.5-mL aliquot of spiked oral fluid and rubbed around for 45 s. The QED A150 was then placed on a flat surface and the applicator inserted into the port with gentle, steady pressure. At this point, a capillary tube was filled, and the oral fluid reached the QA Spot. The background appeared pink when the capillary was filled. The test was completed in 2 min and the device was not moved during this time. After 2 min a purple bar along a printed scale showed the ethanol concentration. The QA Spot also turned purple by this time. Manufacturer instructions state that if the QA Spot was not purple within 5 min from the start of the test, the test is invalid. No tests were invalidated by this criterion.

The manufacturer specified that the test should be administered at least 10 min after eating or drinking and should be performed at an ambient temperature within the range 15 °C to 30 °C. The following compounds are specified not to interfere with the test's operation: ethylene glycol, acetone, methanol, 1-butanol, 2-butanol, 1-propanol, 2-propanol, 1-pentanol, ascorbic acid. However, use of alcohol-containing products, such as mouthwash, cough syrup, breath spray, or chewing tobacco were said to cause elevated results in some cases.

Alco-Screen

The Alco-Screen test is made by Chematics, Inc., and is intended for the semi-quantitative determination of ethanol concentration in oral fluid. The device, consisting of a plastic test strip with a reactive pad at one end, is designed to detect BAC in the range of 0.02 % to above 0.30 % (g ethanol / 100 mL of blood, [units assumed]) ethanol with a reading precision ranging from 0.01 % to 0.1 % depending on the amount of ethanol present. The precision is greater at lower concentrations of ethanol according to the color gradient chart provided with each test. A reactive pad turns gray-green to gray-blue depending on the amount of alcohol present. The ethanol concentration is determined by comparison with a calibrated color chart that is provided. Alco-Screen uses an alcohol oxidase enzyme to oxidize ethanol to acetaldehyde with the accompanied production of hydrogen peroxide, which then reacts with a hydrogen donor (tetramethylbenzidine) to produce a colored product and water. According to the manufacturer, the device responds to methyl, ethyl, and allyl alcohols, but not alcohols with more than 5 carbons or glycine, glycerol, and serine.

The Alco-Screen package was opened just before use and discarded if the test strip was discolored in any way. None of the strips tested were discolored. The reactive pad was saturated with oral fluid for 15 s and a timer started. The color of the reactive pad was observed at 2 min and the results interpreted. The manufacturer warned results might be erroneous after 2 min 30 s. The test was designed to be performed at least 15 min after introducing anything into the mouth and at temperatures less than 80 °F (27 °C) to prevent degradation of the reaction pad. Peroxides and strong oxidizers may enhance color development, while reducing agents, bilirubin, L-dopa, L-methyldopa, and methampyrone may inhibit color development. The manufacturer also warned that the test was sensitive to alcohol vapors and should be performed in an area where these are not present.

Alco-Screen 02

The Alco-Screen 02 test is made by Chematics, Inc., and is intended for the qualitative determination of ethanol concentration in oral fluid. The device, consisting of a plastic test strip with a reactive pad at one end, gives a positive response for samples with a BAC of 0.02 % (g ethanol / 100 mL of blood, [units assumed]) or higher and a negative response in all other cases. A line on the reactive pad turns green in the presence of ethanol; no line appears at ethanol concentrations below 0.02 % (g ethanol / 100 mL of blood, [units assumed]). Alco-Screen 02 uses alcohol oxidase to oxidize ethanol to acetaldehyde with the accompanied production of hydrogen peroxide, which then reacts with a hydrogen donor (tetramethylbenzidine) to produce a colored product and water.

The Alco-Screen 02 package was opened just before use and discarded if the test strip was discolored in any way. None of the strips tested were discolored. The reactive pad was saturated with oral fluid for 15 s and a timer started. After 15 s the device was removed from the spiked oral fluid, and after 10 s more excess spiked oral fluid was shaken from the pad as specified by the manufacturer. The test was completed in 4 min and the distinct green bar indicated a positive result. According to the test maker, after 5 min the result might be erroneous.

The test is subject to many of the same interferences as Alco-Screen, including: peroxides, strong oxidizers, ascorbic acid, tannic acid, pyrogallol, mercaptans, tosylates, uric acid, bilirubin, L-dopa, L-methyldopa, methampyrone, and oxalic acid. However, these are not normally present in human oral fluid in large enough concentrations to be significant according to the manufacturer. Test subjects were not to introduce anything into their mouths for 15 min prior to the test. According to the manufacturer, the device performs best at room temperature and should not be stored above 80 °F (27 °C). Alco-Screen 02 may also be sensitive to alcohol vapors in the air.

Rapid Response Alcohol Test

The Rapid Response Alcohol Test is made by Biotechnostix, Inc., and is intended to determine the presence of alcohol in a single step. The device, consisting of a plastic test strip with a reactive pad at one end, gives a positive response for samples with a BAC of 0.02 % (g ethanol / 100 mL of blood, [units assumed]) or higher and a negative response in all other cases. No information on the chemical basis or specificity of the test was provided by the manufacturer.

The Alcohol Test package was opened just before use and discarded if the test strip was discolored in any way. None of the strips tested were discolored. The reactive pad was saturated with oral fluid for 15 s and a timer started. The result was interpreted after 2 min. A change in color of the reactive pad from light yellow to blue-green (as shown on the foil package) indicated a positive result. As with other devices of this kind, nothing was to be introduced into the mouths of test subjects for 15 min before the test and the device was to be stored between 4 °C to 27 °C.

On Site

The On Site Alcohol testing device is made by Varian, Inc., and is intended for the qualitative determination of ethanol concentration in urine or saliva. The device is a small kit containing a reagent pipet, a urine specimen pipet, a foam pad for collecting oral fluid, and a reaction cassette. It employs a similar alcohol dehydrogenase method as the QED A150. A urine or oral fluid sample is placed onto a chemically treated pad that "volatilizes" reducing alcohols. These vapors are concentrated on a membrane containing an enzyme solution and a tetrazolium salt. When this enzyme-tetrazolium salt comes in contact with ethanol vapor, a formazan dye results, producing a purple + sign.

To administer the test, the foil was peeled back and one drop of reagent from a reagent well was transferred using the reagent pipet to a circle (reagent well) molded on the cassette labeled "results." Then the sample was applied to the sample well using the foam pad that had been saturated with spiked oral fluid for 15 s. The results were interpreted after 2 min.

According to the manufacturer, the On Site test should be performed at least 10 min after eating or drinking to avoid contamination of the oral cavity. The tests should also be performed in a temperature range of 18 °C to 29 °C and the kits stored between 15 °C and 30 °C. The manufacturer stated that the following substances produced no interference when tested at

1.00 % (mass/volume fraction): acetaldehyde, acetone, 2-butanol, ethylene glycol, glycerol and methanol or at 0.10 % (mass/volume fraction): 1-butanol and isopropanol. 1-Propanol gave a faint positive at 0.05 %. Ingestion or general use of over-the-counter medications and products containing alcohol may give a positive result in some cases.

2.3.3 Sensitivity of the Devices: Quantitative Devices

QED A150

Since the QED A150 was designed to give a quantitative response, the testing results for this device were assessed by comparing the ethanol concentration obtained from the device with the ethanol concentration of the spiked oral fluid analyzed simultaneously with the GC-FID. The capillary filled easily with 0.5 mL spiked oral fluid and the QA spot provided an indicator that the test was valid. Bubbles in the capillary made it somewhat more difficult to read the test results at higher concentrations of ethanol. A graph was constructed with the device response plotted along the y-axis and the average ethanol concentration determined by GC-FID plotted on the x-axis (see fig. 1). The slope of this line was 1.06. This is consistent with the value 1.08 reported for the ratio of ethanol oral fluid concentration relative to blood ethanol concentration, (Gubala et al., Pol. J. Pharmacol 2002, 54, 161-165).

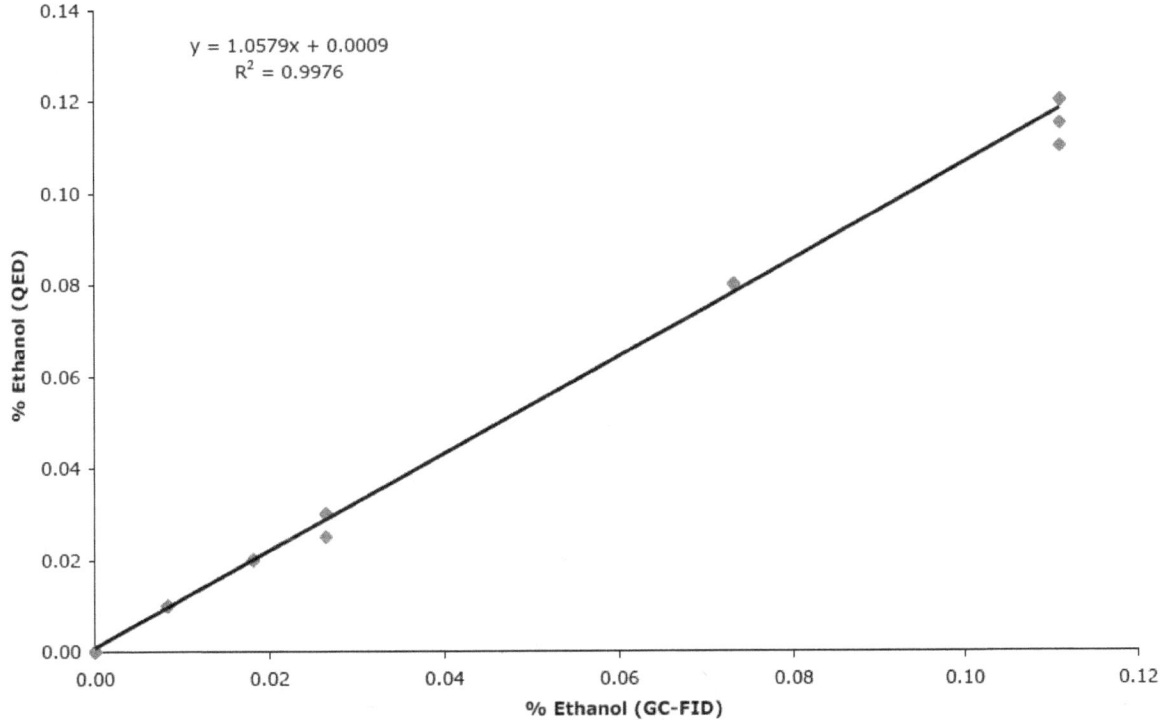

Figure 1. QED A150 Testing Results

Alco-Screen

Because the Alco-Screen device provided a color gradient designed to correspond to various blood alcohol levels, the results for this test were assessed by comparing the ethanol concentration obtained from the device with the ethanol concentration of the spiked oral fluid analyzed simultaneously by GC-FID (see fig. 2). The color chart provided with the device was used to estimate ethanol concentrations. The color of the test strip was matched with, or estimated between, the colors on the chart. The estimated concentrations from the device are plotted on the y-axis of figure 2. The Alco-Screen provided a nonlinear response ($R^2 = 0.61$), with consistently high responses to ethanol in oral fluid. For example, a concentration of about 0.01 % (mass fraction) ethanol gave a color that indicated 0.08 % (mass fraction) ethanol according to the color chart provided.

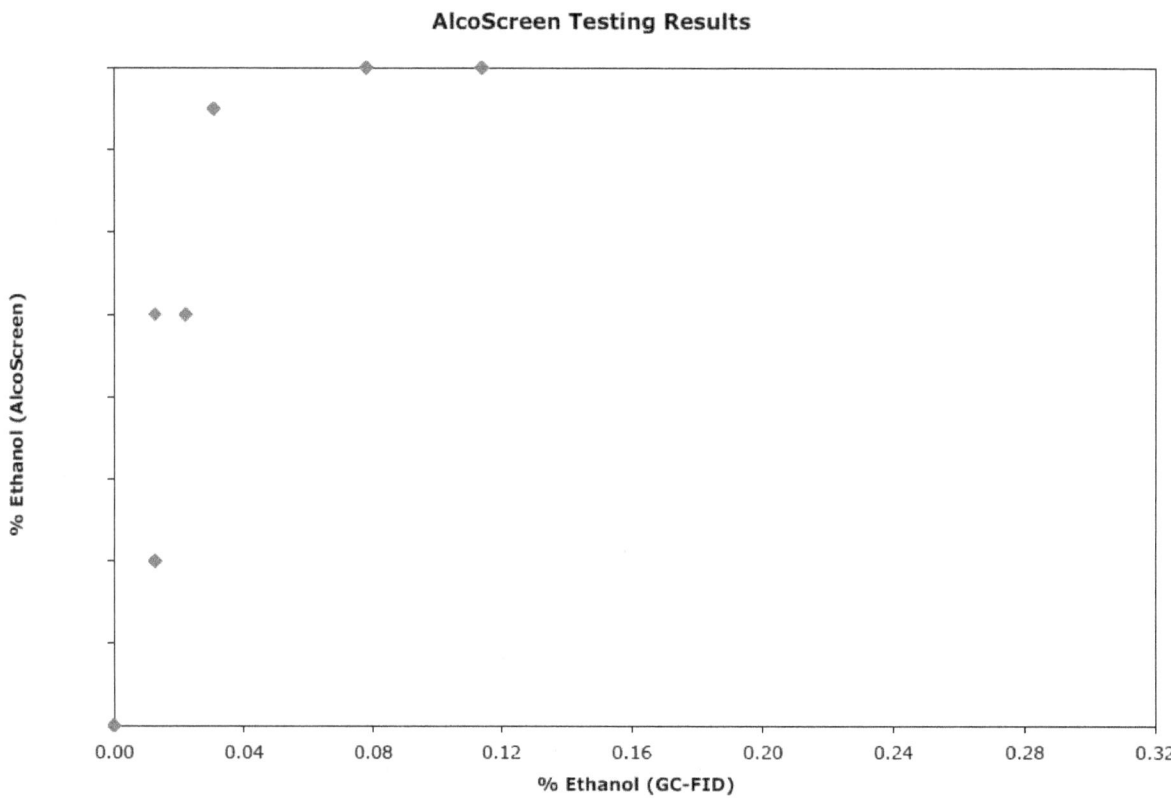

Figure 2. AlcoScreen Testing Results

2.3.4 Sensitivity of the Devices: Qualitative Devices

The response of each of the three qualitative ethanol-test devices was determined to be positive or negative. The response was then characterized as true or false as compared with the % ethanol concentration in spiked oral fluid from the GC-FID tests. Each of these four possible responses was then summed, determining the total number of true positive, false positive, true negative, and false negative responses (see table 1).

12

Table 1. Summary of Results for Qualitative Devices

Device	# tests	# T positives	# F positives	# T negatives	# F negatives
AlcoScreen02	30	20	0	10	0
Rapid Response	30	10	0	10	10
On Site	30	20	0	10	0

Alco-Screen 02

The Alco-Screen 02 response was compared with the % ethanol determined from the spiked oral fluid by GC-FID analysis. The device indicated no false positives or false negatives. The sensitivity, specificity, efficiency, positive predicative value and negative predicative value were all one. The green line that indicated a positive response was lighter at the 0.02 % (mass fraction) limit and increased in intensity as the amount of ethanol increased.

Rapid Response

The Rapid Response alcohol testing device did not provide positive indication of ethanol at concentrations of 0.02 % (mass fraction) or 0.03 % (mass fraction). These false negatives lowered the sensitivity and negative predicative value to 0.5, when compared with the percentage ethanol measured by GC-FID. The efficiency was 0.67, while specificity and positive predicative value were both 1.0. The positive test tended to show a faint green color with blue splotches instead of a fully colored testing pad.

On Site

The On Site device gave a negative response for all tests for the blank and at 0.01 % (mass fraction) ethanol concentration, and a positive response for the higher levels of ethanol. These results meant that the sensitivity, specificity, efficiency, positive predicative value and negative predicative value were all equal to one, when compared with the % ethanol determined by GC-FID. The purple plus symbol was lighter and thinner with lower amounts of ethanol.

2.3.5 Evaluation of Devices with Other Sources of Oral Fluid

To produce the pool of oral fluid used in the studies described above, fresh oral fluid was collected, frozen and thawed twice, and finally centrifuged twice. The supernatant was removed and spiked with aqueous ethanol to produce the spiked oral fluid. In an alternative approach, the aqueous ethanol was added at the outset to pooled oral fluid to see the effect, if any, of processing on the concentration of ethanol. After the addition of ethanol to the oral fluid, the sample was processed as in section 2.2.1. This sample was compared with an oral fluid sample that was spiked with ethanol after processing. Solutions were analyzed in triplicate by GC-FID. The GC-FID results with the two types of oral fluid were not significantly different. The removal of solids, etc., did not seem to affect the determination of ethanol.

Additional tests were performed on the alcohol testing devices using unprocessed oral fluid (directly from the mouth or expectorated). In one test, the swab or the reactive pad was inserted directly into the mouth of a healthy volunteer and clean oral fluid was collected. Each device remained in the mouth for 15 s, except for the QED A150 swab, which remained for 45 s in accordance with manufacturer's instructions. Each device was moved around the cheeks and under the tongue. For the QED A150 it was more difficult to fill the capillary and more bubbles were present than with the pooled and processed oral fluid. No other differences in device performance were observed for the use of pooled and processed oral fluid.

Another test, recently expectorated oral fluid from a healthy volunteer was spiked to a concentration of 0.02 % (mass fraction) and 0.08 % (mass fraction) ethanol. The oral fluid was spiked with the appropriate amount of aqueous ethanol and used immediately for testing. Each of the devices was tested once at both concentrations with accompanying GC-FID analyses. The GC-FID results with unprocessed spiked oral fluid and with processed spiked oral fluid were not significantly different. All of the devices performed similarly with the two sources of oral fluid, except for the Alco-Screen 02, which gave a negative response to the 0.02 % (mass fraction) nominal ethanol concentration.

2.4 Investigation of Interfering Substances

To test how selective each device was toward ethanol, the devices were tested in the presence of four substances that might commonly be found in oral fluid: acetaminophen, L-ascorbic acid, caffeine, and nicotine. While the literature was silent on the concentrations of these substances in oral fluid, common (maximum) levels in blood were available. These values were utilized to set interferent levels in oral fluids. The following concentrations were used in this study: acetaminophen, 25 mg/dL; L-ascorbic acid, 2 mg/dL; caffeine, 2 mg/dL; and nicotine, 3 mg/dL. Each interfering substance was added to aqueous ethanol solutions that were then used to spike clean oral fluid.

2.4.1 Preparation of Solutions for Device Testing

Solutions were prepared to contain 0.1 %, 0.3 % and 0.5 % ethanol (g ethanol/100 g aqueous standard) and interfering substances at levels 10 times the concentrations listed above (12 solutions). After thorough mixing, 15 mL each solution was transferred to a septum-capped vial and stored at 4 °C.

Spiked oral fluid was prepared at nominal ethanol concentrations of 0.01 %, 0.03 %, and 0.05 % (mass fractions) by adding 50 μL of each of these solutions to 0.50 mL aliquots of oral fluid. The resulting 0.55-mL sample was applied directly to the testing device.

Solutions for analysis by GC-FID were prepared as in section 2.2.2. Fresh aliquots of spiked oral fluid and test solutions were prepared each time a device was tested.

2.4.2 Procedure for Testing the Devices

Each of the five devices was tested in triplicate with spiked oral fluid at each of three ethanol concentrations with each interference (described above). A GC-FID analysis accompanied each test. The QED A150 testing swab was placed in the oral fluid for 45 s as specified by the manufacturer. All the other devices were placed in the oral fluid for 15 s to saturate the test pad; saturation with oral fluid was specified by the manufacturers.

2.4.3 Interference Testing Results

Quantitative and Semi-Quantitative Devices

QED A150

Since the QED A150 was designed to give a quantitative response, the testing results for this device were assessed by comparing the ethanol concentration obtained from the device with the ethanol concentration of the spiked oral fluid determined simultaneously by GC-FID. A graph was constructed with the device response plotted along the y-axis and the ethanol concentration from GC-FID plotted along the x-axis (see fig. 3). Lines were constructed for the results with each potential interfering substance added, and for the results without added interference (open squares). Similar results were obtained in the presence and in the absence of the potential interfering substances. A linear relationship between device response and ethanol concentration from GC-FID was apparent in all cases; the R^2 values were 0.99, 0.99, 1.00, and 0.99 for acetaminophen, L-ascorbic acid, caffeine, and nicotine respectively.

QED A150 Interference Testing Results

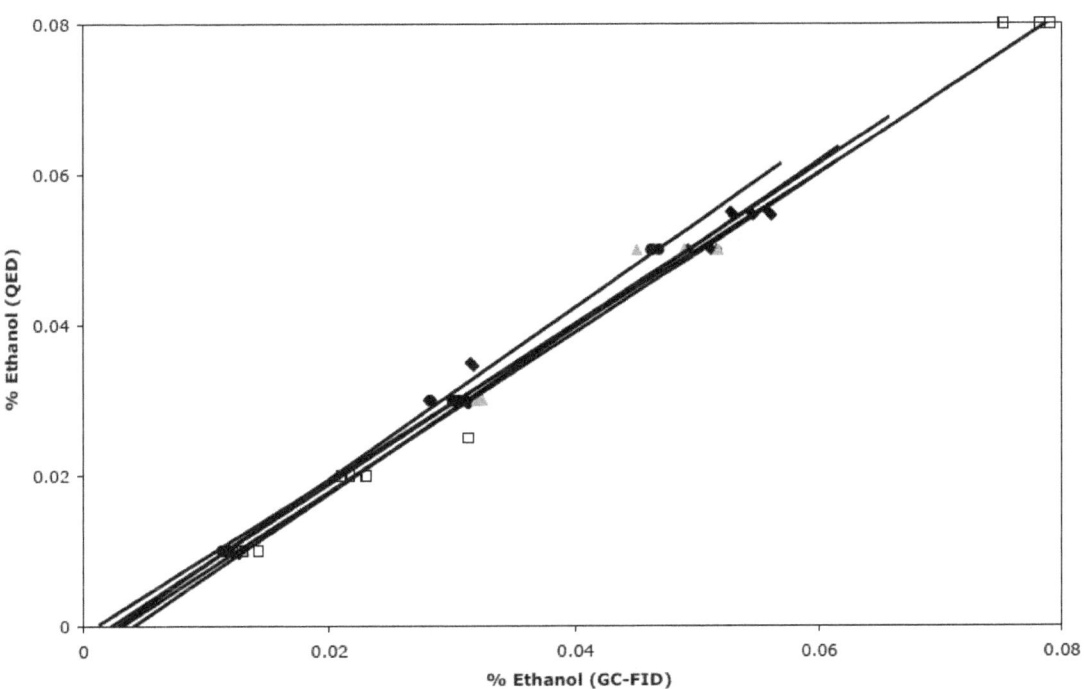

Figure 3. QED A150 Interference Testing Results

15

Alco-Screen

Because the Alco-Screen device provided a color gradient designed to correspond to various blood alcohol level, the results for this test kit were assessed by comparing the ethanol concentration obtained from the device with the ethanol concentration of spiked oral fluid analyzed simultaneously by GC-FID. The color chart provided with the device was used to estimate ethanol concentrations. Results for tests carried out in the presence of potential interferences are shown in figure 4. The device response over a narrow concentration range was more linear than the results of section 2.3.3, with R^2 values of 0.87, 0.97, 0.94, and 0.97 for acetaminophen, L-ascorbic acid, caffeine, and nicotine respectively.

Figure 4. Alco-Screen Interference Testing Results

Qualitative Devices

The response of each of the three qualitative ethanol-test devices was determined to be positive or negative (over or under 0.02 % mass fraction ethanol). The response was then characterized as true or false as compared with the % ethanol in spiked oral fluid from the GC-FID tests. Each of the four possible responses was then summed, determining the total number of true positive, false positive, true negative, and false negative responses (see table 2).

Table 2. Summary of Results for Qualitative Devices with Potential Interferences

Device	# tests	# T positives	# F positives	# T negatives	# F negatives
AlcoScreen02	36	24	0	12	0
Rapid Response	36	23	0	12	1
On Site	36	24	0	12	0

Alco-Screen 02

The Alco-Screen 02 performance was unaffected by the presence of common, potentially interfering substances. The devices showed no false positives or negatives when tested with any of the interfering substances. As such, the sensitivity, specificity, efficiency, positive predicative value, and negative predicative value were all one.

Rapid Response

The Rapid Response test performance was slightly affected by the presence of interfering substances. The detection of ethanol at 0.03 % (mass fraction) was achieved in these tests, contrary to results with unadulterated oral fluid. The Rapid Response device gave a single false negative at 0.03 % (mass fraction) ethanol in the presence of caffeine, and this reduced the sensitivity of the device with caffeine to 0.83, the efficiency to 0.89 and the negative predicative value to 0.75. The values for all other parameters with added caffeine and with the other added substances were one.

On Site

The On Site device appeared to be unaffected by the addition of the four potential interferences. The test provided no false positive or false negative values. This behavior was the same as observed for the On Site device without added substances. The sensitivity, specificity, efficiency, positive predicative value, and negative predicative value were all one for this device.

The selectivity of all of the devices was quite good. None of the potential interferents - acetaminophen, L-ascorbic acid, caffeine, nicotine - at high normal levels caused problems with the tests.

3. DEVICES FOR TESTING FOR DRUGS OF ABUSE

3.1 Experimental

3.1.1 Description of Devices Tested

The point-of-collection drug-testing devices, sources, and catalog and lot numbers are shown in table 3.

Table 3. Point-of-Collection Drug-Testing Devices to be Analyzed

Point-of-Collection Drug-Testing Device	Company	Address	Catalog Number	Lot Number
Oral Fluid Drug Screen Device	Medimpex United Inc.	984 Bristol Pike Bensalem, PA 19020	DOA 5050079	L030200-01
ORAL SCREEN Saliva 4	Craig Medical Distribution Inc.	1185 Park Center Drive, Building P Vista, CA 92081-8305	B52008	032406
iScreen Oral Fluid Device 6	RDI Rapid Detect Inc.	2809 N. Broadway, Suite 7 Poteau, OK 74953	i)DOA5100336 ii)DOA6030435	Lo020241-01
Oratect II	Branan Medical Corporation	10015 Muirlands Road, Suite C Irvine, CA 92618	HM11	G0038

The saliva used in the following analysis was normal human pooled saliva, obtained from Biochemed Services, Winchester, VA 22601 (shown in table 4). The saliva was filtered through a large Buchner funnel into a 500 mL Erlenmeyer flask under vacuum. The saliva was filtered through Whatmann® 541, Hardened Ashless Circles 110 mm filter paper.

Table 4. Pooled Human Saliva

Saliva Batch	Volume	Lot Number
1	1 x 250 mL	BC020106
2	2 x 250 mL	BC031406
3	1 x 250 mL	BC040506
4	1 x 250 mL	BC061406

3.1.2 Sample Preparation

Stock solutions were prepared by dissolving ≈1 mg quantities of each analyte (exact mass known) in 100 mL solvent in a volumetric flask. Acetonitrile was used for solutions of cocaine, and methanol was used in preparation of solutions for all other drugs. These 10 µg/mL solutions were then diluted 1 to 10 to give solutions at 1 µg/mL. Solutions containing isotopically labeled reagents were prepared by a 1:100 dilution of commercially available solutions at a concentration level ≈100 µg/mL. The target analyte, manufacturer and lot number for each drug is shown in tables 5 and 6.

Table 5. Standard Stock Solutions for Target Analytes

Target Analyte	Drug	Lot Number	Manufacturer
Cocaine	Cocaine Hydrochloride	E232019	Mallinckrodt Corporation 675 McDonnell Blvd. Hazelwood, MO 63042
Phencyclidine	Phencyclidine Hydrochloride	40H050	Sigma-Aldrich, Inc. 3050 Spruce Street St. Louis, MO 63103
Codeine	Codeine Sulfate	E277086	Mallinckrodt Corporate 675 McDonnell Blvd. Hazelwood, MO 63042
Morphine	Morphine Free Base	E294032	Mallinckrodt Corporate 675 McDonnell Blvd. Hazelwood, MO 63042
Amphetamine	Amphetamine Sulfate	30H0296	Sigma-Aldrich, Inc. 3050 Spruce Street St. Louis, MO 63103
Methamphetamine	Methamphetamine Hydrochloride	30H0291	Sigma-Aldrich, Inc. 3050 Spruce Street St. Louis, MO 63103
$(\pm)$-11-nor-9-carboxy-Δ^9-tetrahydrocannabinol	Tetrahydrocannabinol Carboxylic Acid	31533-70B	Cerilliant ™ 14050 Summit Drive #121 Austin, Texas 78728

Table 6. Isotopically Labeled Internal Standards for Target Analytes

Target Analyte	Drug	Lot Number	Manufacturer
Cocaine	Cocaine – D_3	30896-13G	Cerilliant ™ 14050 Summit Drive #121 Austin, Texas 78728
PCP	Phen-D_5-cyclidine HCl	5424-M	MSD Isotopes Division of Merck Forest Canada Inc., Montreal, Canada
Codeine	Codeine – D_3 H_2O	1747-P	MSD Isotopes Division of Merck Forest Canada Inc., Montreal, Canada
Morphine	Morphine-D_3 hydrochloride	123H5951	Sigma Chemical Company P.O. Box 14508, St. Louis, MO 63178
Amphetamine	(±)-Amphetamine-D_5	34260-03A	Cerilliant ™ 14050 Summit Drive #121 Austin, Texas 78728
Methamphetamine	(±)-Methamphetamine-D_5	33387-39B	Cerilliant ™ 14050 Summit Drive #121 Austin, Texas 78728
(±)-11-nor-9-carboxy-Δ^9-tetrahydrocannabinol	Tetrahydrocannabinol-D_3 Carboxylic Acid	6341-39	Research Triangle Institute Research Triangle Park, NC 27709-2194

Four sets of saliva samples were prepared for the analysis of the seven target analytes (tables 7-10). Each set of samples consisted of small aliquots of saliva, pipetted into plastic centrifuge tubes and spiked with both the standard solutions and the isotopically labeled internal standard to give approximately 1:1 ratio of analyte to internal standard. Each set of saliva samples contained a range of concentrations to allow LOD for the target analyte to be determined within that particular set.

Table 7. Set 1 – PCP & Cocaine

Concentration (ng/mL)	Vol. of Saliva (mL)	Vol. of PCP stock solution (µL)	Vol. of Cocaine stock solution (µL)	Vol. of PCP-D_5 (µL)	Vol. of Cocaine-D_3 (µL)
50	5	250	250	250	250
40	5	200	200	200	200
30	6.7	201	201	201	201
25	8	200	200	200	200
20	8	160	160	160	160
15	8	120	120	120	120
10	8	80	80	80	80
5	8	40	40	40	40

Table 8. Set 2 – Codeine & Morphine

Concentration (ng/mL)	Vol. of Saliva (mL)	Vol. of Codeine stock solution (µL)	Vol. of Morphine stock solution (µL)	Vol. of Codeine-D_3 (µL)	Vol. of Morhpine-D_3 (µL)
60	5	300	300	300	300
50	5	250	250	250	250
45	5	225	225	225	225
40	5	200	200	200	200
35	5	175	175	175	175
30	5	150	150	150	150
25	8	160	160	160	160
10	8	80	80	80	80
5	8	40	40	40	40

Table 9. Set 3 – Amphetamine (Amph.) & Methamphetamine (M.Amph.)

Concentration (ng/mL)	Vol. of Saliva (mL)	Vol. of Amph. stock solution (µL)	Vol. of M.Amph. stock solution (µL)	Vol. of Amph-D_5 (µL)	Vol. of M.Amph-D_5 (µL)
50	5	250	250	250	250
40	5	200	200	200	200
30	6.7	201	201	201	201
25	8	200	200	200	200
20	8	160	160	160	160
15	8	120	120	120	120
10	8	80	80	80	80
5	8	40	40	40	40

Table 10. Set 4 – Carboxy-THC

Concentration (ng/mL)	Vol. of Saliva (mL)	Vol. of Carboxy-THC stock solution (μL)	Vol. of Carboxy-THC-D₃ (μL)
60	5	300	300
50	5	250	250
40	5	200	200
30	5	150	150
20	8	160	160
12	8	96	96
6	8	48	48

A set of calibrants was made for each set of saliva samples. This enabled the concentration of the target analyte in each solution to be determined by GC/MS (see table 11).

Table 11. Standard Solutions

Ratio of (Unlabelled : Labeled) Standards	Vol. of Unlabelled Solution (μL)	Vol. of Labeled Solution (μL)
1.2:1	480	400
1.1:1	440	400
1.0:1	400	400
0.9:1	360	400
0.8:1	320	400

Solutions were made up for 5 orally administered over the-counter drugs and caffeine. One dose was dissolved in deionized (DI) water and a subsequent aliquot diluted with saliva to give a solution at 0.1 mg/mL. The caffeine solution was made up by dissolving 1 mg of caffeine in 10 mL of saliva. table 12 below shows how the solutions were prepared.

Table 12. Over the Counter Drugs

Target Analyte	Brand Name	Solution A		Solution B		Concentration (mg/mL)
		Quantity in one dose	Vol. of Water	Vol. of Solution A	Vol. of Saliva (mL)	
Acetaminophen	Tylenol	500 mg	100 mL	0.2	10	0.1
Ibuprofen	Advil	200 mg	100 mL (plus 100 mL Ethyl Alcohol 200% proof)	1.0	10	0.1
Aspirin	Aspirin	325 mg	100 mL	0.31	10	0.1
Naproxen Sodium	Aleve	220 mg	100 mL	0.45	10	0.1
Pseudoephedrine	Triaminic Cold & Flu Syrup	15 mg	10 mL	0.67	10	0.1
Caffeine	N/A	N/A	N/A		10	0.1

Solid Phase Extraction

Prior to the solid phase extraction (SPE) of the target analytes from the saliva samples, each SPE method was verified using a solution of the target analyte and water. Two duplicate samples were made up at a concentration of 100 ng/mL. Sample 1 had the internal standard added prior to the extraction taking place. Sample 2 had the internal standard added after the extraction had taken place and prior to drying down by evaporation. The recovery is expressed as a % and was calculated from the measured unlabeled: labeled ratios of sample 1 (S_1) and sample 2 (S_2) using the following formula:

$$\% \text{ Recovery} = (S_2/S_1) \times 100 \hspace{3cm} \text{Eq 6}$$

Solid Phase Extraction of Set 1 (PCP/Cocaine)

Both PCP and cocaine were extracted from the saliva samples in Set 1. 130 mg Bond Elut Certify cartridges (Varian, Inc., Walnut Creek, CA) were used which isolated compounds of interest by non-polar and cation exchange mechanisms. Each saliva aliquot was adjusted to pH 6.0 ($\pm$0.5) by adding 2 mL of phosphate buffer (pH 6.0), and then 100 μL of 1M hydrochloric acid. The column was conditioned with 2 mL methanol and 2 mL 100 mM phosphate buffer (pH 6.0). The sample was loaded onto the cartridge at a rate of 2 mL/min. The loaded cartridge was then washed with 6 mL DI water, and 3 mL 1M acetic acid. The cartridge was then dried by aspiration for 5 min (at 15 KPa) and washed with 6 mL methanol. The PCP and cocaine were eluted from the cartridge with 2 mL methylene chloride/isopropanol/ammonium hydroxide (78/20/2). The eluents were evaporated to dryness with nitrogen at approximately 35 $^{\circ}$C and the analyte was then dissolved in N,O-bis(trimethylsilyl)acetamide (BSA) for GC/MS measurement. The cocaine and PCP are not derivatized by the BSA, but its use as a solvent gives better chromatographic results.

Solid Phase Extraction of Set 2 (Codeine/Morphine)

Both codeine and morphine were extracted from the saliva samples in Set 2. 130 mg Bond Elut Certify cartridges were used to isolate compounds of interest by basic drug extraction with cation exchange and nonpolar mechanisms. Each saliva aliquot was adjusted to pH 8.0 - 8.5 by adding 2 mL of phosphate buffer (pH 8.0). The column was conditioned with 2 mL methanol and 2 mL 100 mM phosphate buffer (pH 8.0). The sample was loaded onto the cartridge at a rate of 2 mL/ min. Then the loaded cartridge was washed with 2 mL DI water, and 2 mL 100 mM acetate buffer (pH 4.0), 2 mL methanol and dried by aspiration for 2 min (at 10 KPa). The codeine and morphine were eluted from the cartridge with 2 mL methanol/ammonium hydroxide (98/2). The eluents were evaporated to dryness with nitrogen at approximately 40 $^{\circ}$C and the analyte was then derivatized with bis(trimethylsilyl)trifluoroacetamide, 99 % with 1 % trimethylchlorosilane (BSTFA with 1 % TMCS).

Solid Phase Extraction of Set 3 (Amphetamine/Methamphetamine)

Both amphetamine and methamphetamine were extracted from the saliva samples in Set 3. 130 mg Bond Elut Certify cartridges were used to isolate compounds of interest by basic drug extraction with cation exchange and nonpolar mechanisms. Each aliquot was adjusted to pH 6.0 (± 0.5) by adding 2 mL of phosphate buffer (pH 6.0). The column was conditioned with 2 mL methanol and 2 mL 0.1 M phosphate buffer (pH 6.0). The sample was loaded onto the cartridge at a rate of 2 mL/min. Then the loaded cartridge was washed with 1 mL 1.0M acetic acid and dried by aspiration for 5 min (at 15 KPa). The cartridge was then washed with 6 mL methanol and dried aspiration for 2 min (at 10 PKa). The amphetamine and methamphetamine were eluted from the cartridge with 2 mL methylene chloride/isopropanol/ammonium hydroxide (78/20/2). The eluents were evaporated to dryness with nitrogen at approximately 35 °C and the analyte was then derivatized with heptafluorobutyric acid anhydride (HFAA).

Solid Phase Extraction of Set 4 (Carboxy-THC)

Carboxy-THC was extracted from the saliva samples in Set 4. 130 mg Bond Elut Certify cartridges were used to isolate the compound of interest by hydrophobic interactions; interferences were removed by ion exchange and secondary polar interactions. Each saliva aliquot was adjusted to pH 4.0 by adding 5 mL of 100 mM acetate buffer (pH 4.0). The column was conditioned with 2 mL methanol and 2 mL 50 mM phosphoric acid. The sample was loaded onto the cartridge at a rate of 2 mL/min. Then the loaded cartridge was washed with 9 mL 50 mM phosphoric acid, 3 mL 50 mM phosphoric acid/methanol (80/20) and then dried by aspiration for10 min (at 15 KPa). The cartridge was then washed with 200 μL hexane. The carboxy-THC was eluted from the cartridge with 1 mL hexane/ethyl acetate (80/20). The eluents were evaporated to dryness with nitrogen at approximately 40 °C and the analyte was then derivatized with BSTFA with 1 % TMCS.

3.1.3 GC/MS Analysis

The following conditions were set for all the analyses carried out by GC/MS. The GC injector was heated to 270 °C and transfer line to 280 °C. Helium was used as the carrier gas with a head pressure of 15 psi. Samples were introduced by splitless injection, with the split valve opened at 0.75 min. The mass spectrometer was operated in the electron ionization mode with ionization energy of 70 eV. The samples were introduced with an autosampler through an HP5890 series II gas chromatograph. Table 13 shows the temperature parameters and the target ions for each analyte.

Table 13. GC/MS Temperature Parameters and Target Ions for Individual Analytes

Target Analyte	Ions	Initial Temp (°C)	Initial Time (min)	Rate (°C /min)	Final Temp (°C)	Rate (°C /min)	Final Temp (°C)	Hold Time (min)	Rate (°C /min)	Hold Temp (°C)	Hold Time (min)	Run Time (min)
Cocaine PCP	182/185 200/205	150	1.0	25	250	10	285	1.5	15	300	2.0	13
Codeine Morphine	371/374 429/432	150	1.0	25	250	10	285	2.5	25	300	1.0	12.6
Amphetamine Methamphetamine	240/244 254/258	120	1.0	5	150	0	0	2.0	30	300	1.0	15
Carboxy-THC	371/374	120	0.5	5	150	25	250	0.5	10	300	3.0	13

Selected ion chromatograms for each target analyte (*fig. 5-11*) are in the appendix section.

25

The following protocol was used when analyzing all four sets of saliva samples. Single analyses of each of the five standards were run followed by analyses of samples within the set in ascending order of concentration. The samples were then run in descending order, followed by the analysis of the five standards in reverse order. By combining the data of the standards run before and after the samples, a composite linear regression ($y = mx + b$) was calculated for each of the target analytes, which was used to convert the measured intensity ratios of analytes to weight ratios. The weight ratios were then used along with the amounts of internal standards added to calculate the analyte concentration in each sample.

3.1.4 Device Test Procedures

All the devices evaluated utilize lateral flow chromatographic immunoassays. These devices work via the same principles, utilizing monoclonal antibodies to selectively detect elevated levels of specific drugs in human oral fluid. Each device was tested with 4 sets of saliva samples until a LOD could be determined for each analyte. The devices varied in the volume of saliva required to run the test, the time taken to read the test results, and the analytes detected. Table 14 shows the various criteria for the individual tests.

Table 14. Criteria for Oral Fluid Drug Testing Devices

Oral Fluid Drugs Testing Device	Volume of Saliva Required	Designated dropping area	Read Results after	Analyte(s) detected
Oral Fluid Drug Screen Device	5 drops per well	2 adjacent wells	10 min	PCP, Cocaine, Codeine, Morphine, Amphetamine, Methamphetamine, Carboxy-THC.
ORAL SCREEN Saliva 4	4 drops	1 well	15 min	Cocaine, Codeine, Morphine, Methamphetamine, THC.
iScreen Oral Fluid Device 6	15 drops	1 well	10 min	PCP, Cocaine, Codeine, Morphine, Amphetamine, Methamphetamine, Carboxy-THC.
iScreen Oral Fluid Device 6	30 drops	Plastic cup	10 min	PCP, Cocaine, Codeine, Morphine, Amphetamine, Methamphetamine, Carboxy-THC.THC
Oratect II	15 drops	Cotton tip	5 min	PCP, Cocaine, Morphine, Amphetamine, Methamphetamine, Carboxy-THC.THC

3.2 Device Testing Results

Oral Fluid Drug Screen Device

The Oral Fluid Drug Screen Device is very compact (7 cm x 4 cm) and has spaces available to record both the date and the identification of the sample being tested. The kit has two wells in which the sample is placed (5 drops per well) and two corresponding windows in which the test results could be viewed. Window one indicated the presence or absence of cocaine, methamphetamine and PCP and window two, THC, opiates and amphetamine. This particular device did not differentiate between codeine and morphine; it only detected the group opiates. Each window has a control line which is required to be present in order for the test results to be validated. Each detection window is labeled with the target analyte. A negative result is shown by the presence of a pink line next to the named target analyte, indicating that the analyte is not present in the sample at concentrations above or equal to its LOD. A positive result is shown by the absence of a pink line next to the target analyte, indicating that the analyte is present in the sample at a concentration equal to or greater than its LOD. Table 15 shows the limit of detection obtained for each analyte and the manufacturers claimed limit of detection. The results from the analysis are subject to interpretation. Upon a consensus of two people, the LOD for both cocaine and PCP was 5 ng/mL lower than the manufacturer's claimed value. The lines for the opiates were very faint and at times difficult to determine. The LOD for opiates was determined at 5 ng/mL higher than the manufacturer's claimed value. Amphetamine, also showing very faint lines for a negative result, had an LOD as claimed by the manufacturer, whereas the LOD for methamphetamine was 20 ng/mL less than the claimed value. Carboxy-THC results showed the greatest variance from the manufacturer's claims with an LOD 28 ng/mL higher than claimed. It was also noted that the lines for carboxy-THC were consistently faint throughout analysis. Because the determination of results is open to interpretation by the individual analyst, the differences between the manufacturer's claims and the results are insignificant, with the exception of carboxy-THC.

Table 15. Limit of Detection for Analytes using Oral Fluid Drug Screen Device

Target Analyte	LOD (ng/mL)	Manufacturer's LOD (ng/mL)
Cocaine	15	20
PCP	5	10
Codeine	45	40
Morphine	45	40
Amphetamine	50	50
Methamphetamine	30	50
Carboxy-THC	40	12

Oral Screen Saliva 4

The Oral Screen Saliva 4 was also compact (2.5 cm x 10 cm) but only detected 4 analytes; THC, cocaine, opiates, and methamphetamine. The device had a space for the ID of the sample to be recorded, a single well for introduction of saliva (4 drops), and a viewing window to observe the results. This device worked in the same manner as the Oral Fluid Drug Screen Device in that the presence of a control line was required to validate the test, the appearance of a pink line indicated a negative result, and the absence of the pink line indicated a positive result. Table 16 shows the LOD's obtained for each of the 4 target analytes and the manufacturers claimed LOD's. These results represent a consensus of two people. The LOD for both opiates and carboxy-THC were the same as the manufacturers claimed value. The LOD for cocaine was 10 ng/mL lower and the LOD for methamphetamine was 10 ng/mL higher than the given values. Differences between the manufacturer's claimed LOD values and the test results are insignificant due to the possible differences in interpretation of results. With the exception of the opiate, line all the lines on this test kit were very clear and easy to read. The opiate line, however, was very faint when no opiates were present, and results would be subject to interpretation depending on the particular analyst.

Table 16. Limit of Detection for Analytes using ORAL SCREEN Saliva 4

Target Analyte	LOD (ng/mL)	Manufacturer's LOD (ng/mL)
Cocaine	5	15
PCP	N/A	N/A
Opiates	10	10
Amphetamine	N/A	N/A
Methamphetamine	60	50
Carboxy-THC	50	50

iScreen Oral Fluid Devices

During the analysis of the iScreen Oral Fluid Devices a second batch was ordered. When the second batch was received it became apparent that the manufacturer had altered the outer casing surrounding the assay component.

a) Set A (3.25 cm x 10 cm) utilized large well in which 15 drops of saliva were to be applied.
b) Set B (93 cm x 12 cm) utilized sponge applicator which was to be soaked in 30 drops of saliva to reach saturation.

Both devices tested for 6 analytes; cocaine, methamphetamine, PCP, THC, opiates, and amphetamines via the same basic principles. We found cocaine, PCP, codeine, and morphine all had LOD values lower than the manufacturers claimed value, 15 ng/mL, 5 ng/mL, 20 ng/mL, and 20 ng/mL respectively. Methamphetamine was found to have the same LOD value while amphetamine and carboxy-THC had higher LOD values by 10 ng/mL and 8 ng/mL respectively. Because of possible difference in interpretation, the differences between our recorded LOD values and those claimed by the manufacturer were small and were considered to be insignificant. The lines for both amphetamine and methamphetamine were consistently very faint for this drug testing device. As a result of this, interpretation was difficult and subject to large uncertainties (see table 17).

Table 17. Limit of Detection for Analytes using iScreen Oral Fluid Device 6

Target Analyte	LOD (ng/mL)	Manufacturer's LOD (ng/mL)
Cocaine	5	20
PCP	5	10
Codeine	20	40
Morphine	20	40
Amphetamine	60	50
Methamphetamine	50	50
Carboxy-THC	20	12

Oratect II

The Oratect II (1.75 cm x 13 cm) provides a space for both the date and the sample ID to be recorded. It detects six analytes; methamphetamine, carboxy-THC, cocaine, amphetamine, opiates, and PCP. The device consists of a sponge pad at the end where the saliva is to be applied (15 drops) and two windows to view the test results. There is also a plastic cover to put over the sponge pad once the saliva has been applied to it. The carboxy-THC and amphetamine lines were found to be extremely faint with the Oratect II. Cocaine and morphine both had LOD's lower than the claimed value, 10 ng/mL and 30 ng/mL respectively. The LOD for PCP was as claimed and methamphetamine and carboxy-THC both had higher LOD's by 25 ng/mL and 60 ng/mL respectively. The Oratect II failed to produce a positive result for all concentrations of amphetamine tested. A lack of positive result for amphetamine and the dramatically increased LOD for carboxy-THC are significantly different from the manufacturer's claimed LOD values (see table 18).

Table 18. Limit of Detection for Analytes using Oratect II

Target Analyte	LOD (ng/mL)	Manufacturer's LOD (ng/mL)
Cocaine	10	20
PCP	5	4
Codeine	N/A	N/A
Morphine	10	40
Amphetamine	>100	25
Methamphetamine	50	25
Carboxy-THC	100	40

3.3 Interference Testing

Each of the devices were tested for cross reactivity with 5 over the-counter drugs and with caffeine, a substance commonly found in human saliva (shown in table 19). Solutions were made at 100 µg/mL and evaluated using the test kits. Acetaminophen, ibuprofen, aspirin, naproxen sodium, and caffeine all produced negative test results for all analyte classes and thus no further testing was carried out. Pseudoephedrine produced a positive result with for all 4 devices and testing was repeated using a more dilute solution, 10 µg/mL. The results from this analysis were negative for all devices and for all analyte classes.

Table 19. Results from Cross Reactivity Testing

	Oral Fluid Drug Screen Device	ORAL SCREEN Saliva 4	iScreen Oral Fluid Device 6	Oratect II
Acetaminophen 100μg/mL	Negative for all analytes	Negative for all analytes	Negative for all analytes	Negative for all analytes
Ibuprofen 100 μg/mL	Negative for all analytes	Negative for all analytes	Negative for all analytes	Negative for all analytes
Aspirin 100 μg/mL	Negative for all analytes	Negative for all analytes	Negative for all analytes	Negative for all analytes
Naproxen Sodium 100 μg/mL	Negative for all analytes	Negative for all analytes	Negative for all analytes	Negative for all analytes
Caffeine	Negative for all analytes	Negative for all analytes	Negative for all analytes	Negative for all analytes
Pseudoephedrine 100 μg/mL	Positive for Amphetamines & Methamphetamine	Positive for Methamphetamine	Positive for Amphetamines & Methamphetamine	Positive for Amphetamines & Methamphetamine
Pseudoephedrine 10 μg/mL	Negative for all analytes	Negative for all analytes	Negative for all analytes	Negative for all analytes

3.4 Results from GC/MS Analysis

Method linearity is defined by results that are directly proportional to analyte concentration within a given range. The linearity for each method was established by plotting the response ratio (analyte response/internal standard response) against the actual weight ratio (analyte concentration/internal standard concentration). The fit parameter (R^2) is an indicator of the linearity of the data. The R^2 values for each analyte is shown in table 20 along with the % recovery values for each analyte.

Table 20. R^2 Values and % Recovery for the 7 Analytes

Analyte	R^2 Value	Recovery
Cocaine	0.988	95 %
PCP	0.999	95 %
Codeine	0.999	103 %
Morphine	0.996	93 %
Amphetamine	0.971	92 %
Methamphetamine	0.989	90 %
Carboxy-THC	0.977	46 %

3.5 Summary of Results

It is important to acknowledge that the manufacturers of each point-of-collection drug-testing kit state within the instruction sheet that the assay provides only a preliminary analytical test result. A more specific alternate chemical method must be used for confirmation. Gas chromatography/ mass spectrometry (GC/MS) and gas chromatography/tandem mass spectrometry (GC/MS/MS) are the two preferred confirmatory techniques. In general, the ability of each of the kits to detect drugs of abuse at relatively low concentrations (ng/mL) was good. The size of the kits and the ease of carrying out each test would allow use in a wide variety of environments. A few discrepancies in the interpretation of the results were apparent, and these discrepancies would be exacerbated in poor working conditions that might be encountered in field use (e.g., poor lighting conditions).

Small discrepancies were also apparent between the LOD's determined for each analyte and the LOD value claimed by the manufacturer. In general, these discrepancies were of minor significance. Due to the subjective nature of the interpretation of results, small discrepancies in results are to be expected.

If the LOD is equal to or lower than claimed by the manufacturer, (i.e., more sensitive than claimed), lower levels of drugs will be detected. As indicated by manufacturers it is essential that all positive results are confirmed by GC/MS or GC/MS/MS. Higher LOD's result in false negatives, which occur when the kits are less sensitive than stated, such discrepancies are of much greater concern.

THC-COOH was the most difficult analyte to detect. The observed LOD was higher than the manufacturer's LOD by a factor of 2.5 for Oratect II, by a factor of 3 for the Oral Fluid Drug Screen Device, and by a factor of 1.3 with iScreen Oral Fluid Device. For the Oratect II devices, limits of detection for amphetamine were >4 times higher than claimed, and LODs for methamphetamine were 2 times higher than claimed. In all of these cases false negative results would be obtained.

APPENDIX

0

Figure 5. Selected ion Chromatograms by GC/MS for Phencyclidine and Phen-D$_5$-cyclidine

0

Figure 6. Selected ion Chromatograms by GC/MS for Cocaine and Cocaine-D₃

33

0

Figure 7.   Selected ion Chromatograms by GC/MS for Codeine and Codeine-D$_3$

0

Figure 8. Selected ion Chromatograms by GC/MS for Morphine and Morphine-D₃

0

Figure 9. Selected ion Chromatograms by GC/MS for Amphetamine and Amphetamine-D₅

0

Figure 10. Selected ion Chromatograms by GC/MS for Methamphetamine and Methamphetamine-D$_5$

0

Figure 11.   Selected ion Chromatograms by GC/MS for Tetrahydrocannabinol Carboxylic Acid and Tetrahydrocannabinol-D₃.carboxylic Acid

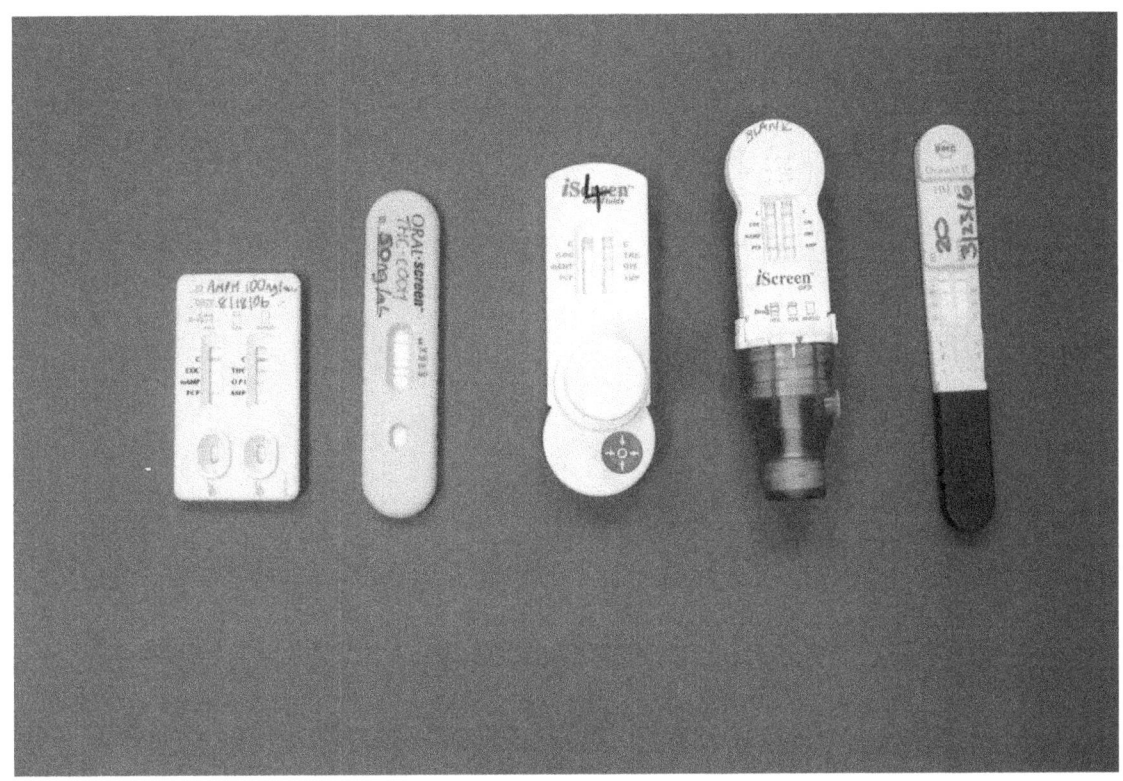

1.   2.   3.   4.   5.

Figure 12. Point of Collection Oral Fluid Drug Testing Devices

Table 21. Point of Collection Oral Fluid Drug Testing Devices and the Results Shown in Figure 12

	Point of Collection Drug Testing Device	**Saliva Spiked with**	**Concentration**	**Positive Result(s)**	**Negative Result(s)**
1.	Oral Fluid Drug Screen Device	Amphetamine Methamphetamine	100 ng/mL	Amphetamine Methamphetamine	All other analytes
2.	Oral Screen 4	Carboxy -THC	50 ng/mL	Carboxy -THC	All other analytes
3.	iScreen	Cocaine PCP	25 ng/mL	Cocaine PCP	All other analytes
4.	iScreen	Blank Saliva	N/A	None	All Analytes
5.	Oratect II	Methadone Codeine	20 ng/mL	Methadone Codeine	All other analytes